PICTURE A COUNTRY

Egypt

Henry Pluckrose

W
FRANKLIN WATTS
A Division of Grolier Publishing
NEW YORK • LONDON • HONG KONG • SYDNEY
DANBURY, CONNECTICUT

This is the Egyptian flag.

First published by Franklin Watts in 1998
First American edition 1998 by
Franklin Watts
A Division of Grolier Publishing
90 Sherman Turnpike
Danbury, CT 06816

Visit Franklin Watts on the Internet at:
http://publishing.grolier.com

Library of Congress Cataloging-in-Publication Data
Pluckrose, Henry Arthur.
    Egypt / Henry Pluckrose.
       p. cm. -- (Picture a country)
    Includes index.
    Summary: A simple introduction to the geography, people,
culture, and interesting sites of Egypt.
    ISBN 0-531-11506-2 (lib. bdg.)   0-531-15362-2 (pbk.)
    1. Egypt--Juvenile literature. [1. Egypt] I. Title.
II. Series: Pluckrose, Henry Arthur. Picture a country.
DT49.P58 1998   98-11291
962--DC21   CIP
                                                  AC

Series editor: Rachel Cooke
Series designer: Kirstie Billingham
Picture research: Juliet Duff
Printed in Great Britain

Photographic acknowledgments:

Cover: Robert Harding Picture Library t, Eye Ubiquitous
cr (Paul Stewart), Getty Images cr (Werner Otto),
Travel Ink b (Abbie Enock).

AA Photo Library p. 16;
J. Allan Cash pp. 11t, 28;
Axiom Photographic Agency pp. 8 & 23 (James Morris),
13, 14, 19 & 24 (Alex Misiewicz);
James Davis Travel Photography p. 29t;
Eye Ubiquitous p. 21 (Paul Stewart);
Getty Images pp. 10 (Werner Otto), 18, 22b;
Robert Harding Picture Library pp. 9, 11b, 12, 15 (Nigel
Francis), 17, 22t, 26, 27;
Travel Ink pp. 25, 29 (Abbie Enock)
Chirstine Osborne Pictures pp. 20.

All other photography Steve Shott.
Map by Julian Baker.

Contents

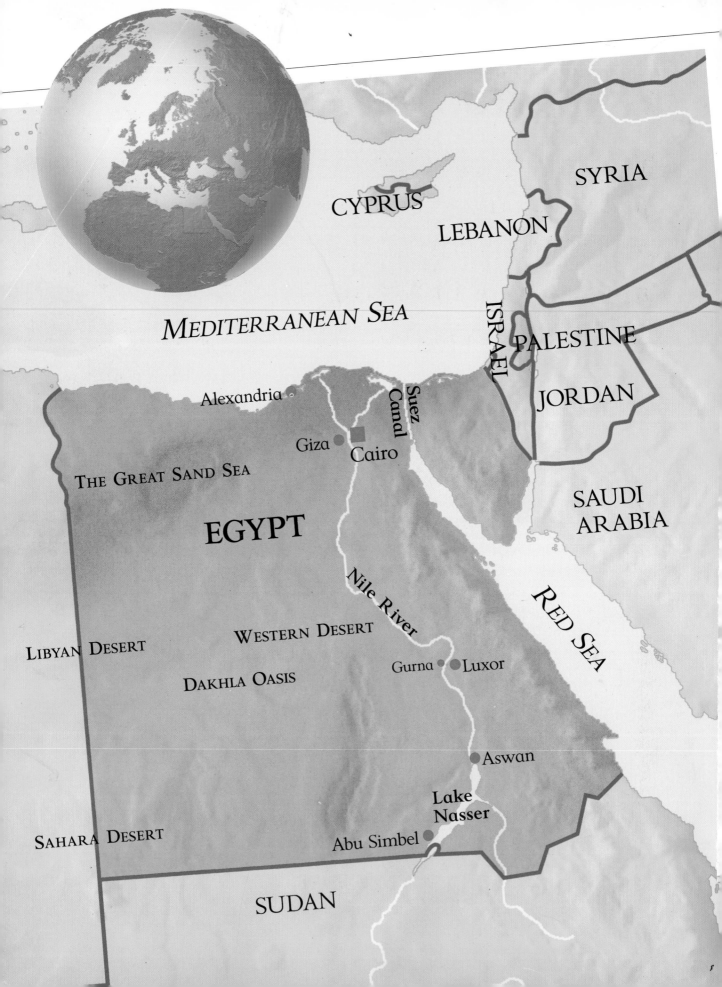

Where Is Egypt?

This is a map of Egypt.
Egypt is a country in which
two continents meet.
Part of Egypt is in Africa;
part of Egypt is in Asia.

Here are some
Egyptian stamps
and money.

Egyptian money
is counted in pounds.

The Egyptian Landscape

Egypt is a country of deserts.

A desert is a place where very little rain falls.

Deserts are usually very hot or very cold.

In Egypt, the deserts are hot
because the sun shines all day.

But, at night, they become a lot colder.

Deserts do not all look the same. This is part of Egypt's Western Desert called the White Desert.

The Nile is the longest river in the world. It is 4,037 miles (6,497kms) long. This is the Nile at Aswan.

The Nile River runs through Egypt.
It is very important because it brings water to the land along its banks.

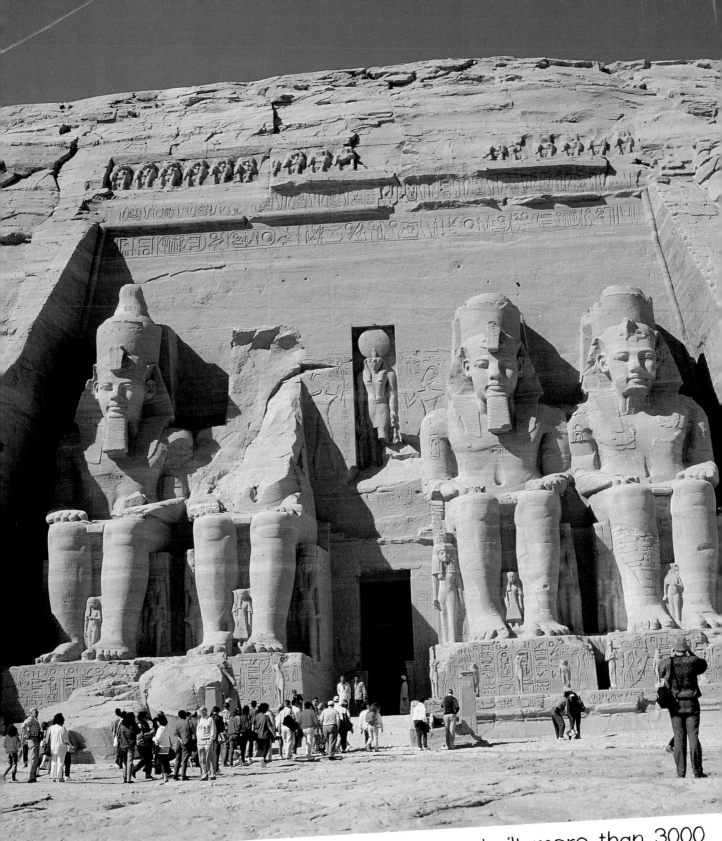

This great temple at Abu Simbel was built more than 3000 years ago, when the pharaoh Ramses II ruled Egypt.

The Egyptian People

People have lived in Egypt for thousands of years.
They lived along the Nile River and
built cities, villages, palaces, and temples.

The streets of Egyptian cities are always
filled with people. This street is in Luxor.

Today, more than 60 million
people live in Egypt.
They speak and write Arabic.

Where They Live

Most Egyptians live in towns and villages along the Nile River.

In the village of Gurna on the Nile, houses are painted to celebrate pilgrimages to Mecca, the Muslims' sacred city.

Alexandria is on the Mediterranean coast of Egypt. Today, it is a busy, modern city.

The city of Alexandria is Egypt's largest port. It was founded and named by Alexander the Great, the Greek king who conquered Egypt in 332 B.C.

The Capital City

Cairo is the capital of Egypt.
More than 16 million people live there.
It is an old city but also modern.
You will find many new buildings
alongside older ones.

This is a clothes market in a
street in old Cairo.

Like most of Egypt's towns and cities, Cairo is built on the banks of the Nile River.

Canals and Dams

The Suez Canal runs across Egypt.
It joins the Mediterranean to the Red Sea
and the Indian Ocean.
It was built so that great ships could travel
between Europe and Asia without going
around Africa. Ships pay to use the canal.

The Suez Canal cuts straight through the desert.
It is 92 miles (148 km) long and was opened in 1869.

The Aswan dam was built in the 1960s.
The dam formed a huge lake called Lake Nasser.

An enourmous dam was built across the
Nile at Aswan. The dam controls the
amount of water flowing through the river.
The water flowing through the dam is used
to make electricity.

Farming

Egyptian farmers grow many
crops along the Nile Valley.
They grow corn, rice, sugarcane, cotton,
fruits, vegetables, olives, and grapes.
They keep goats, cattle, sheep, and chickens.

This is the Dakhla Oasis in the Western Desert. More than 15,000 people live in some of Egypt's oasis towns.

Farmers can also grow crops at oases in the desert.

An oasis (plural "oases") is a place in the desert where water bubbles up from under the ground.

19

Family Life

Many Egyptian families
work on small farms.
Their homes are in country villages
or towns.

This Egyptian family is eating a meal. The mother
covers her head, like many Egyptian women.

This is a Bedouin man with his children. Bedouin men often wear red-and-white cloths on their heads.

Some of the people of Egypt are nomads, who do not always live in one place. They are called Bedouins. They have a home that moves with them — a tent.

Egyptian Food

Egyptians enjoy all sorts of different foods.
They eat round, flat cakes of bread
with each meal.

This is a dish of
stuffed grape leaves.

This woman is baking flat Egyptian bread.

This market stall is selling a selection of baklava and other sweet treats.

Egyptians like kebabs, which are cubes of meat cooked on a stick. They enjoy fish, fried bean cakes called ta'maia, rice, goat's cheese, and sweet pastry called baklava, which contains nuts and honey.

Out and About

Egyptians take part in water sports — fishing, scuba diving, windsurfing, and sailing.

The Red Sea is full of coral reefs. Scuba divers like to explore the reefs, which are full of colorful fish.

These posters are advertising Egyptian films.
The films are usually full of action and adventure.

They like to watch weight-lifting and
wrestling competitions.
People also go to see camel racing.
The cinema is very popular in Egypt, and
a lot of films are made there each year.

Mosques and Festivals

Egypt is an Islamic country.
This means that most Egyptians are Muslims
and follow the teachings of Mohammed.
Muslims go to the mosque to worship God.

People go to pray at the Mohammed Ali mosque in Cairo.

Mawlid is a religious carnival with snake charmers, prancing horses, and dancers.

Each year, the Egyptians have religious festivals that often celebrate things to do with their daily lives, like fishing and horses.

Visiting Egypt

If you go to Egypt, you might go down
the Nile River by boat to visit
the temples and pyramids built by
the ancient Egyptians.

The pyramids are
tombs built for the
pharaohs of ancient
Egypt. This is the
Great Pyramid at Giza.

This boat takes tourists down the Nile. The boat is like a floating hotel. People eat and sleep on it.

You might explore a bazaar —
a market where you can find bags,
belts, pots, jewelry,
rugs, and blankets.
You might even try to
buy a camel!

Index

About This Book

The last decade of the 20th century has been marked by an explosion in communications technology. The effect of this revolution upon the young child should not be underestimated. The television set brings a cascade of ever-changing images from around the world into the home, but the information presented is only on the screen for a few moments before the program moves on to consider some other issue.

Instant pictures, instant information do not easily satisfy young children's emotional and intellectual needs. Young children take time to assimilate knowledge, to relate what they already know to ideas and information that are new.

The books in this series seek to provide snapshots of everyday life in countries in different parts of the world. The images have been selected to encourage the young reader to look, to question, to talk. Unlike the TV picture, each page can be studied for as long as is necessary and subsequently returned to as a point of reference. For example, forms of Egyptian dress might be compared with their own; a discussion might develop about the ways in which food is prepared and eaten in a country whose culture and customs are different from their own.

The comparison of similarity and difference is the recurring theme in each of the titles in this series. People in different lands are superficially different. Where they live (the climate and terrain) obviously shapes the sort of houses that are built, but people across the world need shelter; coins may look different, but in each country people use money.

At a time when the world seems to be shrinking, it is important for children to be given the opportunity to focus upon those things that are common to all the peoples of the world. By exploring the themes touched upon in the book, children will begin to appreciate that there are strands in the everyday life of human beings that are universal.